AF428244

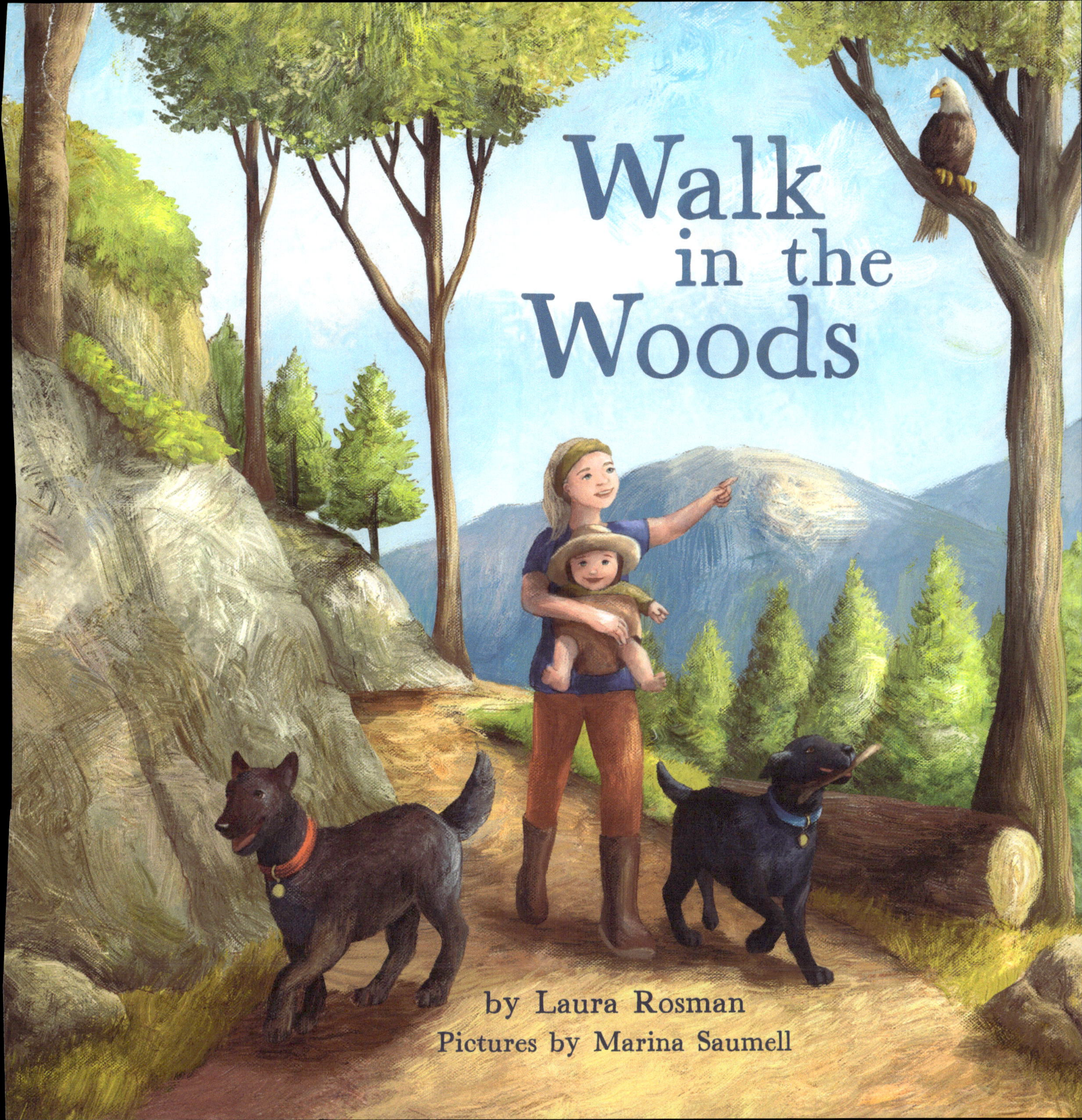

Walk
in the
Woods
by Laura Rosman
Pictures by Marina Saumell

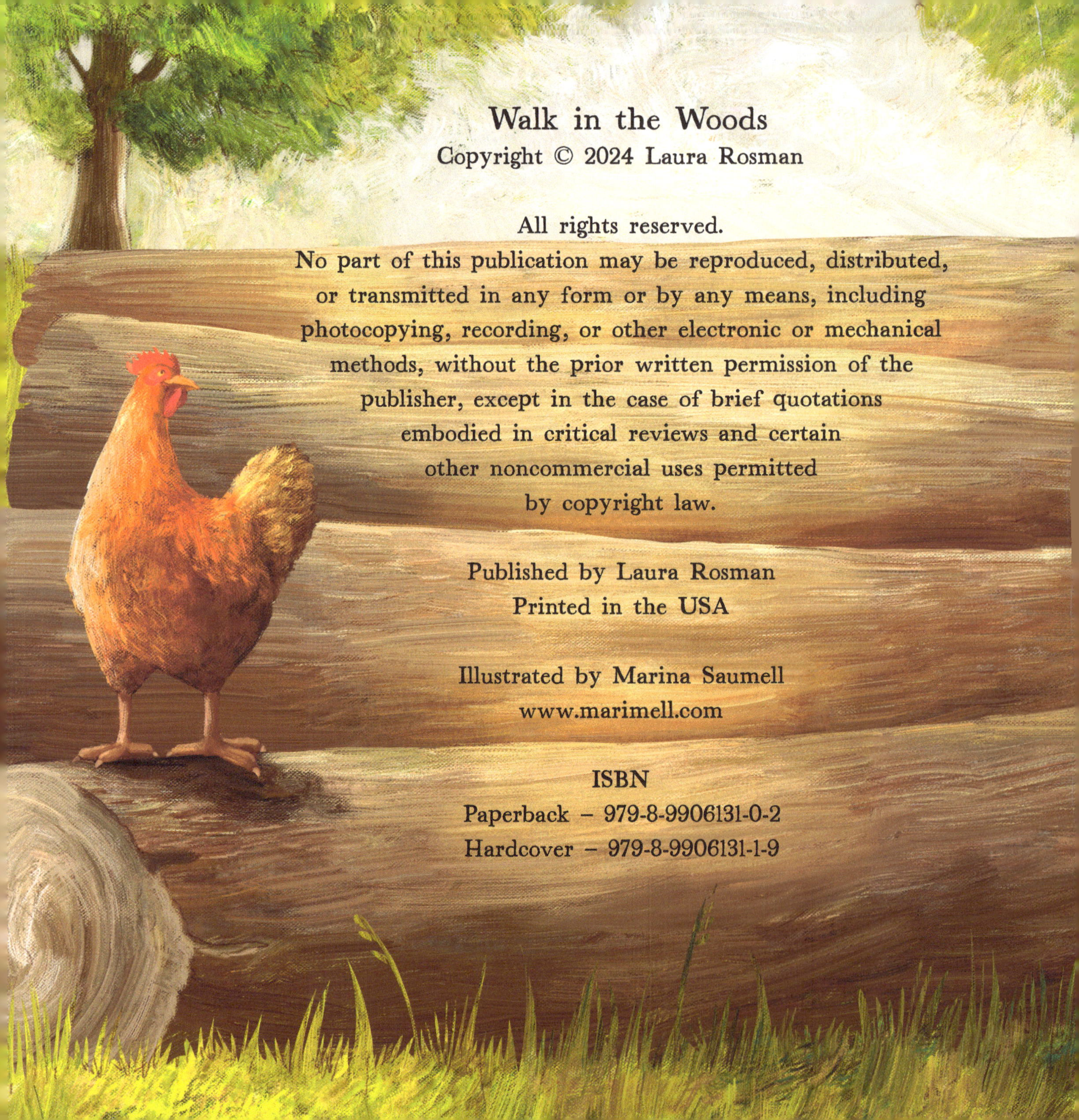

Walk in the Woods
Copyright © 2024 Laura Rosman

Published by Laura Rosman
Printed in the USA

Illustrated by Marina Saumell
www.marimell.com

ISBN
Paperback — 979-8-9906131-0-2
Hardcover — 979-8-9906131-1-9

This book is dedicated to Sawyer.
Thank you for every walk through our woods.
I hope you continue to go off trail,
hug all the trees, find the best walking stick
and throw the biggest stones.

This book belongs to

Sawyer and Mom walking in the woods
Every day, walking in the woods
Checking out the sky
Checking out the ground
Checking out the animals
Checking out the sounds

Tasting the wild berries
Counting all the ants
Climbing on the slippery rocks
Digging up all the plants

Sawyer and Mom walking in the woods
Every day, walking in the woods
Checking out the sky
Checking out the ground
Checking out the animals
Checking out the sounds

Playing in the dirt
Chatting about our day
Singing with the birds
Watching the dogs play

Sawyer and Mom walking in the woods
Every day, walking in the woods
Checking out the sky
Checking out the ground
Checking out the animals
Checking out the sounds

Grooming all the trails
Putting on our gear
Trekking through the snow
Scoping out the deer

Sawyer and Mom walking in the woods
Every day, walking in the woods
Checking out the sky
Checking out the ground
Checking out the animals
Checking out the sounds

Smelling all the flowers
Learning about new trees
Listening to the creek
Picking up all the leaves

Sawyer and Mom walking in the woods
Every day, walking in the woods
Checking out the sky
Checking out the ground
Checking out the animals
Checking out the sounds

Feeding our wild chickens
Making castles in the sand
Cutting wood for all our projects
Building on our land

Sawyer and Mom walking in the woods
Every day, walking in the woods
Checking out the sky
Checking out the ground
Checking out the animals
Checking out the sounds

THINGS YOU MAY FIND IN THE WOODS
Put the name and ✓ when you find them.

ABOUT THE AUTHOR

After years of trying to have a child and struggling with infertility, Laura decided to become a stay at home mom after having her daughter. It was a difficult adjustment, so she decided to make it her mission to get outside every day and walk in their woods while carrying her daughter. The fresh air, sounds of nature and sense of freedom gave Laura a new purpose in life and created a bond between mom and daughter that would only grow.

Laura began to write this song on her daily walks about their time together and would sing it to her daughter every day.

Laura is an avid runner, outdoor enthusiast and hiker. She loves spending her time with her husband, daughter and dogs on their property in Upstate New York.

ABOUT THE ILLUSTRATOR

Marina Saumell graduated with a degree in architecture in 2003 and embarked on a career in commercial architecture. The birth of her child and growing love of children's books inspired her to venture into book illustration. Since 2006, Marina has joyously followed her passion for drawing and illustration.

She has illustrated more than 50 children's books, engaging all kind of audiences from early readers to young adults.